Dedicated to Myles

This is a book about the koala...

About things you might not be aware.

For example a koala...

Is NOT a BEAR!

The koala is a marsupial...

Australia is their habitat...

Koalas are mammals...

I bet you already knew that!

Baby koalas are called joeys...

Yes, it's the same as a baby kangaroo...

Both joeys are born without fur...

Lucky their mom's pouch keeps them warm through and through!

Koalas sleep most of the day...

A eucalyptus diet doesn't improve their energies...

As nocturnals they move around more in the night...

And they mostly sleep in trees...

And now it's time to JUMP JUMP JUMP...

And SNORE, SNORE, SNORE LIKE A KOALA!

The word koala means
NO DRINK...

All the water they need comes from leaves...

Living near their food source is good for napping...

And when there are droughts or heat waves.

Koalas are capable climbers...

Using the strength of their arms and their claws...

When frightened they bound up a tree very fast...

They go up, not down like Santa Claus!

You might wonder if koalas have thumbs like we do...

And yes, it's true!

On their front paws they have two!

Imagine if we had extra thumbs what we could do!

And now it's time to JUMP JUMP JUMP...

And SNORE, SNORE, SNORE JUST LIKE A KOALA!

Koalas look cute and cuddly...

But they might not be quite awake!

So if you hear them snoring...

Don't wake them for goodness sake!

Koalas don't need to hibernate...

Since they already sleep most of the day!

Snuggled high up in a tree...

Where the wind can't blow them away!

Joeys live in their mother's pouch...

For nearly half a year...

Then she gives them a piggyback...

Until the joey's first birthday nears.

Let's sing
HAPPY BIRTHDAY!

Happy First Birthday!

Happy Birthday dear joey to you!

And now it's time to JUMP JUMP JUMP

Then SNORE, SNORE, SNORE, JUST LIKE A KOALA!

WE

KOALA

SNORES!

Jump Series:

Jump Like a Caribou!
Jump Like a Kangaroo!
Jump at the Zoo!
Jump and Say P.U.!
Jump and Say Boo!
Jump and Say Valentine's Day Is
For Kids Too!
Jump and Look For a Clue!
Jump and Say Happy Birthday to You!
Jump For Everything Blue!
Jump, Hop and Say Happy Easter To You!
Jump and Say Cock-A-Doodle-Do!
Jump and Sing Da-Do-Do-Do!
Jump and Ask Who? Who?
Jump and Squawk Like a Cockatoo!
Jump and Ask Is It You or Ewe?
Jump and Say There's an Ewww in My Stew!
Jump and Say Merry Christmas To You!
Jump and Cheer Happy New Year!
Jump and Say There's a Moo-Moo in a Tutu!
Jump and Say There's a Hare in My Hair!
Jump and Say My Aunt Ate An Ant!
Jump and Say There's An Aardvark
In The Amusement Park!

Jump and Roar For The Dinosaurs!
Jump and Buzz Like A Bee!
Jump and Flutter Like A Butterfly!
Jump and Pop Like Popcorn!
Jump and Ribbit Like A Frog!

Clap For Series
Clap for 1!
Clap for 2!
Clap for 3!
Clap for 4!
Clap for 5!
Clap for 6!
Clap for 7!
Clap for 8!
Clap for 9!
Clap for 10!

The Cat Who Said Hello
The Three Boulders
Billy Shakespeare/Billie Shakespeare
Learn To Draw With Symmetry
ABC More Learn to Draw With Symmetry

Non-Fiction
103 Fundraising Ideas For Parent Volunteers With
Schools and Teams